You
are

By Andrew East

DEDICATION:

To my Mom and Dad
who allowed me to believe that
anything is possible and to my wife
who has shown me this.

Did you know you are
very special, one of a kind?

I wanted to tell you some of the
things in you I find

You are brave as a lion,
you have no fear
And as happy as a cat
who loves to dance and cheer

You are as smart as
the wisest owl
And strong as a bear
with a big growl

You change like a caterpillar
to a butterfly
And you are kind to everyone,
every creature nearby

You are as
curious as a
little fish
And you are very
very ticklish!

You always work hard, a
very busy beaver
And you are a better giver
than receiver

You leave things better
than they were found
And take good care of
everything around

So with all of this that has been given to you
Let me tell you about the things you can DO

You can jump
or you can dance
You can ride a horse
and have it prance

You can run really fast
and pictures you can draw
You can make animals noises...
"oink oink" and "hee haw"

You can talk a lot
or talk a little
You can play the drums
or pluck the fiddle

You can play games
and you can do puzzles
And I hope that you give lots
and lots of cuddles

And don't ever forget what I always say
You will be loved every single day

You can bike
or you can
skate
You can shovel
or you can
rake

You can camp
or you can
boat
You can swim
or you can
float

You can sing your
favorite song
And make others feel
like they belong

You can giggle
or you can smile
Just be nice
and respectful
all the while

Just work hard
and do things right
Know that your love and laughter
can be a light

And if you have a
tough time, that's okay
You will still be hugged
at the end of the day

So when you grow
big and go on adventures afar

Just remember
all the things
that you are.

the end

www.ingramcontent.com/pod-product-compliance
Lightning Source LLC
Chambersburg PA
CBHW042027090426
42811CB00016B/1773

* 9 7 8 0 5 7 8 6 6 9 2 3 6 *